Travel Journal

Spain

VPJournals

Contact Details

Name:

Email address:

Tel:

Address:

Important Medical Information

Blood type:

Medication:

CONTENTS

Hi, I hope you enjoy this journal. It is packed with cool stuff and recommendations for you trip to Spain, and has plenty of space to record details of your trip.

What's Inside	Page
Before you go to Spain	
Great places to visit in Spain	6-7
Cool places to visit in Spain with kids	8-9
Good places to eat	10-11
Research Spain	12-13
Postcard & Packing List	14-19
Spain facts	21-22
Helpful hints	23-26
Clothes and shoe sizing charts, to help you get the right sizes while there	
Spain Trip Diary	27-111
21 day trip diary to record details of your trip	
Reflect on you Trip	
Summary of your trip	113-121
People you met	123-125
Useful Resources	127-136
Size conversion charts	129-132
Common Translations	133-134
Notes	135-136

Have fun in Spain

Great Places to visit in Spain

Parque de la Naturaleza de Cabarceno	✓
Faunia	
Basilica of the Sagrada Familia	
Casa Batllo	
Mercat de Sant Josep de la Boqueria	
Museo de Altamira (Cueva de Altamira)	
Gothic Quarter (Barri Gotic)	
Loro Parque	
Click Mallorca	
Palace of Catalan Music	
Playa de Ses Illetes	
Las Ramblas	

Hammam Al Andalus Granada	
Palau Guell	
Playa de las Catedrales	
Parc de Montjuic	
Retiro Park (Parque del Retiro)	
Museo del Romanticismo	
Guggenheim Museum Bilbao	
Cerralbo Museum	
Royal Palace of Madrid	
Plaza de Espana	
Palmitos Park	
Museu Europeu d'art Modern - MEAM	
Prado Museum	

Cool Places to visit in Spain with Kids

Park Guell	✓
Zoo Aquarium de Madrid	
Parque de la Naturaleza de Cabarceno	
PortAventura	
Aquopolis	
Siam Park	
Aquopolis Costa Dorada	
Palma Aquarium	
Rancho Texas Lanzarote Park	
Oasis Park Fuerteventura	
Selwo Marina Delfinarium	
Magic Fountain (Font Magica)	

Terra Mitica	
Camp Nou	
Costa Caribe Aquatic Park	
Aquopolis Sevilla	
Aquopolis San Fernando de Henares	
Aquopolis Cullera	
Oceanografic	
Costa Martianez	
Barcelona Zoo	
CosmoCaixa Barcelona	
Aqualandia	
Ciudad de las Artes y las Ciencias (City of Arts and Sciences)	

Good Places to Eat in Spain

Torres Bermejas	✓
Kokoro	
Asador Real	
Rincon de Roque	
Cerveceria Plaza Mayor	
Restaurant Botin	
Abrasador	
El Celler de Can Roca	
El Club Allard	
FADO Restaurante Portugues	
Cerveceria Catalana	
Cera 23	

Eslava	
Con Gracia	
Navarro	
Restaurant Montiel	
Ciudad Condal	
Dassa Bassa	
ABaC Restaurant	
Arzak	
Restaurante Con Alma	
Los Montes de Galicia - Azcona	
Restaurante Arume	
7 Portes	
Saaron	

Best Websites to Research Further

Do some more research on the internet to plan your trip:

www.wikipedia.org/wiki/Spain
www.spain.info
www.lonelyplanet.com/spain
www.esmadrid.com/en/
www.barcelonaturisme.com
www.tourspain.org
www.barcelona-tourist-guide.com/
www.spain-tenerife.com
www.nomadicmatt.com/travel-guides/Spain-travel-tips/

More places I want to visit on our trip

1. _____

2. _____

3. _____

4. _____

5. _____

6. _____

7. _____

8. _____

9. _____

10. _____

11. _____

12. _____

13. _____

14. _____

15. _____

Postcard List

Name:
Address:

Name:
Address:

Name:
Address:

Name:

Address:

Name:

Address:

Name:

Address:

Name:

Address:

Name:

Address:

Name:

Address:

Name:

Address:

Name:

Address:

Name:

Address:

Name:

Address:

Name:

Address:

MAIL

Packing List

✓	This Journal
	Tickets
	Passport
	Money
	Chargers
	Batteries
	Book to read
	Camera
	Tablet
	Sun glasses
	Sun cream

	Toiletries
	Water
	Watch
	Snacks
	Umbrella
	Towel
	Guide book
	Kindle
	Jacket
	Medication
	Add more below

Spain Facts

- The name Spain diverged from the word "Ispania", which means the "land of rabbits"

- There are four official languages in Spain: Castilian Spanish, Catalan, Galician and Basque

- Mount Teide is the highest mountain in Spain (3,718 m, 12,198 ft) and is an active volcano

- The Pyrenees is a mountain range that divides Spain and France

- There is no tooth fairy in Spain but rather a tooth mouse called Ratoncito Perez who exchanges children's teeth for gifts

- Real Madrid, the Spanish football club based in Madrid, is the most valuable sports team in the world

- Spain is home to a type of tailless monkey, the macaque, which is the only type of wild monkey that lives in Europe

- Flamenco is a Spanish folk music and dance from the region of Andalusia in southern Spain

- There is a Spanish New Year custom called Twelve Grapes. Spaniards celebrate the New Year by eating one grape with their family for each bell strike of the clock (for a total of 12 grapes)

- Euskera, spoken by the Basque population in northern Spain and southern France, is one of the oldest living languages in the world.

- Spain is home to the world's largest tomato fight: La Tomatina, celebrated every year in Valencia

- The Madrid subway is the second largest underground system in Europe and the sixth largest system in the world.

- Spain is the number one producer of olive oil in the world with 44% of the world's olive oil production. The largest Olive Oil producing region is Andalucia.

- The oldest known cave painting is found in the Cave of El Castillo in northern Spain. There researchers have found a faint red dot that is thought to be over 40,000 years old.

- Seat is the only Spanish car brand.

Clothes & Shoe Sizes

Children's Shoe Sizes

UK	EUROPE	US	Japan
4	20	4½ or 5	12 ½
4 ½	21	5 or 5½	13
5	21 or 22	5½ or 6	13 ½
5 ½	22	6	13½ or 14
6	23	6½ or 7	14 or 14½
6 ½	23 or 24	7 ½	14½ or 15
7	24	7½ or 8	15
7 ½	25	8 or 9	15 ½
8	25 or 26	8½ or 9	16
8 ½	26	9½	16 ½
9	27	9½ or 10	16 ½ or 17
10	28	10½ or 11	17 ½
10½ or 11	29	11½ or 12	18
11 ½	30	12½	18 or 18 ½
12	31	13	19 or 19 ½
12 ½	31	13 or 13½	19 ½ or 20
13	32	1	20
13 ½	32 ½	1 ½	20 ½
1	33	1½ or 2	21
2	34	2½ or 3	22

Children's Clothing Sizes

UK	EUROPE	US	Australia
12m	80cm	12-18m	12m
18m	80-86cm	18-24m	18m
24m	86-92cm	23-24m	2
2-3	92-98cm	2T	3
3-4	98-104cm	4T	4
3-5	104-110cm	5	5
5-6	110-116cm	6	6
6-7	116-122cm	6X-7	7
7-8	122-128cm	7 to 8	8
8-9	128-134cm	9 to 10	9
9-10	134-140cm	10	10
10-11	140-146cm	11	11
11-12	146-152cm	14	12

Women's Shoe Sizes

UK	EUROPE	US	Japan
3	35 ½	5	22 ½
3 ½	36	5 ½	23
4	37	6	23
4 ½	37 ½	6 ½	23 ½
5	38	7	24
5 ½	39	7 ½	24
6	39 ½	8	24 ½
6 ½	40	8 ½	25
7	41	9 ½	25 ½
7 ½	41 ½	10	26
8	42	10 ½	26 ½

Women's Clothes Sizes

UK	US	Japan	France / Spain	Germany	Spain	Australia
6/8	6	7-9	36	34	40	8
10	8	9-11	38	36	42	10
12	10	11-13	40	38	44	12
14	12	13-15	42	39	46	14
16	14	15-17	44	40	48	16
18	16	17-19	46	42	50	18
20	18	19-21	48	44	52	20

Men's Shoe Sizes

UK	EUROPE	US	Japan
6	38 ½	6 ½	24 ½
6 ½	39	7	25
7	40	7 ½	25 ½
7 ½	41	8	26
8	42	8 ½	27 ½
8 ½	43	9	27 ½
9	43 ½	9 ½	28
9 ½	44	10	28 ½
10	44	10 ½	28 ½
10 ½	44 ½	11	29
11	45	12	29 ½

Men's Suit / Coat / Sweater Sizes

UK / US / Aus	EU / Japan	General
32	42	Small
34	44	Small
36	46	Small
38	48	Medium
40	50	Large
42	52	Large
44	54	Extra Large
46	56	Extra Large

Men's Pants / Trouser Sizes (Waist)

UK / US	Europe
32	81 cm
34	86 cm
36	91 cm
38	97 cm
40	102 cm
42	107 cm

We have included another copy of this at the back of the book, so you can find it quickly again when you are in Spain

Spain Trip Diary

Write a daily diary during your trip

Day 1

Date: _____   **Weather:** _____

_____

_____

_____

_____

_____

_____

_____

_____

_____

_____

_____

_____

_____

_____

Day 2

Date: _____   **Weather:** _____

Day 3

Date: _____   **Weather:** _____

_____

_____

_____

_____

_____

_____

_____

_____

_____

_____

_____

_____

_____

_____

Day 4

Date: _____ **Weather:** _____

Day 5

Tip! Send your postcards

Date: _____   Weather: _____

_____

_____

_____

_____

_____

_____

_____

_____

_____

_____

_____

_____

_____

_____

_____

44

Day 6

Date: _____   **Weather:** _____

Day 7

Date: _____   **Weather:** _____

_____

_____

_____

_____

_____

_____

_____

_____

_____

_____

_____

_____

_____

_____

_____

_____

Day 8

Date: _____   **Weather:** _____

Day 9

Date: _____   **Weather:** _____

Day 10

Date: _____   **Weather:** _____

Day 11

Date: _____   **Weather:** _____

Day 12

Date: _____   **Weather:** _____

Day 13

Date: _____   Weather: _____

_____

_____

_____

_____

_____

_____

_____

_____

_____

_____

_____

_____

_____

_____

_____

_____

_____

Day 14

Date: _____   **Weather:** _____

Day 15

Date: _____   **Weather:** _____

Day 16

Date: _____   **Weather:** _____

_____

_____

_____

_____

_____

_____

_____

_____

_____

_____

_____

_____

_____

_____

Day 17

Date: _____   **Weather:** _____

Day 18

Date: _____   **Weather:** _____

Day 19

Date: _____ **Weather:** _____

Day 20

Date: _____   **Weather:** _____

_____

_____

_____

_____

_____

_____

_____

_____

_____

_____

_____

_____

_____

_____

_____

Day 21

Date: _____   **Weather:** _____

_____

_____

_____

_____

_____

_____

_____

_____

_____

_____

_____

_____

_____

_____

Memories of your Trip

Things I will remember from the trip

Favorite Places visited on the Trip

People I Met

Name:
Address:
Tel:
email:

Name:
Address:
Tel:
email:

Name:
Address:
Tel:
email:

Name:
Address:
Tel:
email:

Name:
Address:
Tel:
email:

Name:
Address:
Tel:
email:

Name:
Address:
Tel:
email:

Name:
Address:
Tel:
email:

Name:
Address:
Tel:
email:

Name:
Address:
Tel:
email:

Name:
Address:
Tel:
email:

We hope you enjoyed your trip to Spain

Please leave us a review if you found this Journal useful

Check out our useful resources on the next few pages

Clothes & Shoe Sizes

Children's Shoe Sizes

UK	EUROPE	US	Japan
4	20	4½ or 5	12 ½
4 ½	21	5 or 5½	13
5	21 or 22	5½ or 6	13 ½
5 ½	22	6	13½ or 14
6	23	6½ or 7	14 or 14½
6 ½	23 or 24	7 ½	14½ or 15
7	24	7½ or 8	15
7 ½	25	8 or 9	15 ½
8	25 or 26	8½ or 9	16
8 ½	26	9½	16 ½
9	27	9½ or 10	16 ½ or 17
10	28	10½ or 11	17 ½
10½ or 11	29	11½ or 12	18
11 ½	30	12½	18 or 18 ½
12	31	13	19 or 19 ½
12 ½	31	13 or 13½	19 ½ or 20
13	32	1	20
13 ½	32 ½	1 ½	20 ½
1	33	1½ or 2	21
2	34	2½ or 3	22

Children's Clothing Sizes

UK	EUROPE	US	Australia
12m	80cm	12-18m	12m
18m	80-86cm	18-24m	18m
24m	86-92cm	23-24m	2
2-3	92-98cm	2T	3
3-4	98-104cm	4T	4
3-5	104-110cm	5	5
5-6	110-116cm	6	6
6-7	116-122cm	6X-7	7
7-8	122-128cm	7 to 8	8
8-9	128-134cm	9 to 10	9
9-10	134-140cm	10	10
10-11	140-146cm	11	11
11-12	146-152cm	14	12

Women's Shoe Sizes

UK	EUROPE	US	Japan
3	35 ½	5	22 ½
3 ½	36	5 ½	23
4	37	6	23
4 ½	37 ½	6 ½	23 ½
5	38	7	24
5 ½	39	7 ½	24
6	39 ½	8	24 ½
6 ½	40	8 ½	25
7	41	9 ½	25 ½
7 ½	41 ½	10	26
8	42	10 ½	26 ½

Women's Clothes Sizes

UK	US	Japan	France / Spain	Germany	Spain	Australia
6/8	6	7-9	36	34	40	8
10	8	9-11	38	36	42	10
12	10	11-13	40	38	44	12
14	12	13-15	42	39	46	14
16	14	15-17	44	40	48	16
18	16	17-19	46	42	50	18
20	18	19-21	48	44	52	20

Men's Shoe Sizes

UK	EUROPE	US	Japan
6	38 ½	6 ½	24 ½
6 ½	39	7	25
7	40	7 ½	25 ½
7 ½	41	8	26
8	42	8 ½	27 ½
8 ½	43	9	27 ½
9	43 ½	9 ½	28
9 ½	44	10	28 ½
10	44	10 ½	28 ½
10 ½	44 ½	11	29
11	45	12	29 ½

Men's Suit / Coat / Sweater Sizes

UK / US / Aus	EU / Japan	General
32	42	Small
34	44	Small
36	46	Small
38	48	Medium
40	50	Large
42	52	Large
44	54	Extra Large
46	56	Extra Large

Men's Pants / Trouser Sizes (Waist)

UK / US	Europe
32	81 cm
34	86 cm
36	91 cm
38	97 cm
40	102 cm
42	107 cm

Common Translations

English	French	Spanish	Italian
Hello	Bonjour	Hola	Ciao
Goodbye	Au revoir	Adiós	Arrivederci
Yes	Oui	Sí	Si
No	Non	No	No
Please	S'il-vous-plaît	Por favor	Per favore
Thank you	Merci	Gracias	Grazie
Excuse me	Excusez-moi	Perdón	Mi scusi
How much	Combien	Cuánto	Quanto
My name is	Mon nom est	Mi nombre es	Io mi chiamo
Where is	Où est	Dónde está	Dov'è
The bank	La banque	El banco	La banca
The toilet	Les toilettes	El baño	Il bagno

German	Japanese	Mandarin	Hindi
Hallo	Kon'nichiwa	Ni hao	Namaste
Auf Wiedersehen	Sayonara	Zaijian	Alavida
Ja	Hai	Shi de	Ham
Nein	Ie	Meiyou	Nahim
Bitte	Onegaishimasu	Qing	Krpaya
Vielen Dank	Arigato	Xiexie	Dhan'yavada
Entschuldigung	Sumimasen	Duoshao	Mujhe mapha karem
Wie viel	Ikura	Wo de mingzi shi	Kitana
Mein Name ist	Watashinonamaeha	Nali	Mera nama hai
Wo ist	Doko ni aru	Yinhang	Kaham hai
Die Bank	Ginko	Yinhang	Bainka
Die Toilette	Toire	Cesuo	Saucalaya

Notes: